I0435223

What To Do - If You Find A Baby Bird On The Ground

2014

By Lucinda Choules

Cover Photo by Gwen Bailey

by Lucinda Choules

Graduate Student
Stephen F. Austin State University, Nacogdoches, TX.

BS Animal Science, Texas State University, San Marcos, TX.

BAS Food Science & Technology, University of Ballarat, VIC AU.

Volunteer Bird Rehabilitator

Copyright 2014 USA
Published by Lucinda Choules at **CreateSpace**

ISBN-13: 978-1500448837
ISBN-10:1500448834

TABLE OF CONTENTS

CHAPTER 1

(Figure 1) Lost baby?

Photo by Brigitte Werner (2012)

WHAT TO DO FIRST?

First - determine whether or not the baby is being cared for by its parents. If the baby is covered with feathers like the robin above, it is a fledgling just learning to fly and the baby is likely not orphaned. The parents will continue to feed the baby wherever he winds up during his flying trials including: on the ground, in bushes, or in branches.

The baby may appear abandoned but that does **not** mean that he is really lost. The parent may be keeping a watchful eye over his adventures from a nearby tree. Therefore, before removing him from the area, go inside and watch the baby from the window.

If your child brought the baby into the house; ask where they found the bird. Then place the fledgling in an area away from cats, near where he was found; and watch from a window inside the house. If the baby is still being cared for the parent will eventually appear; feed him an insect or two, and leave again in search of more.

If the baby does not have feathers; it has likely fallen out of a nest. Try to locate the nest by placing the baby on the ground near where you found it. The baby will make a beacon type "chirping" noise, listen for that same noise in the nearby trees.

Please note- most birds have a poor sense of smell; so the parents will not know that you have held the baby (that is an old-wives tale). It is my observation that even if you place the baby in the nest in full view of the mother or place it under her; she still will not reject the baby.

(Figure 2) To find the nest - look for grasses or twigs surrounding tree branches.

Photo by Deluna (2012)

If you find the nest, before placing the baby back in it, check to make sure that a baby cowbird is not in the nest. Cowbirds practice brood parasitism; which means that they trick other birds into raising their young for them. The parent cowbird lays an egg in another usually much smaller song birds' nest. This egg hatches a day earlier, allowing the baby to quickly grow larger than its' foster siblings. The larger cowbird chick demands more food and attention from the parents and crowds out the natural siblings sometimes dropping them out of the nest.

If you put the baby back in with the cowbird; it will likely be knocked out again. Cowbird babies are huge compared to the other natural babies in the nest; and when they gape you can see a white lining to the red inside of the mouth.

Other songbirds may also have a red mouth with a white lining so it is not always easy to tell if the baby is a cowbird by this fact alone. But, if two babies in the nest are small with yellow inside of the mouth and one is large with red in the mouth; that clearly shows that you have a cowbird issue. Ask your rehabber what to do with the cowbird chick, remove it from the nest, and place the natural baby back in the nest.

If no cowbirds are present and the baby appears unharmed place it back in the nest. If the baby is injured; you should take it to a veterinarian before putting it back in the nest.

IF YOU ARE UNABLE TO FIND THE NEST OR PARENTS

If you find the nest, but it is broken or smashed; you can try making a nest out of a small basket lined with tissues or paper towels. Hang the basket from a tree away from cats and other predators. Then watch to see if the parent finds and cares for the baby in the makeshift nest.

Be careful where you place this nest, because ants are an issue and can kill baby birds. The nest should be placed on a small branch above the ground, and check to make sure no ant hills or mounds surround the tree.

If your makeshift nest does not work; you cannot find the original nest; or you know the parents are dead because- they flew into a window in front of you, or your cat brought them in and dropped them at your feet. Then you need to find a rehabilitator to take the baby.

Finding your local rehabber is not always easy, below are some websites that can help in your search.

LOCATING A REHABILITATOR

America

Wild Care's - Animal Rehabilitators list is a very comprehensive source of information - This link is run by the University of Minnesota at www.tc.umn.edu and Wild Care at wildcarebayarea.org. It provides – Animal rehabilitator information for all 50 states.
http://www.wildcarebayarea.org/site/DocServer/11-30-10_correction.html?docID=381

Audubon Society recommends the following website which also lists rehabbers by state:
http://wildliferehabber.com/rehabber-search you can contact your local chapter of the National Audubon Society 1-212-979-3000 or (800) 274-4201 9:00 am - 9:00 pm for further information. www.audubon.org./

Humane Society - phone: 202-452-1100 (from North America, 866-614-4371). Monday—Friday 8:00 a.m. to 11:00 p.m., Saturday— Sunday 9:00 a.m. - 6:00 p.m., ET. Their webpage lists ways to find a rehabber. http://www.humanesociety.org/animals/resources/tips/find-a-wildlife-rehabilitator.html

Local Parks and Wildlife Offices -list rehabbers by county. For instance, if you live in TX contact TPWD: http://www.tpwd.state.tx.us/huntwild/wild/rehab/list/ Each state has its own Parks and Wildlife office so search for yours by state.

US Fish and Wildlife at 1-800-344-WILD (1-800-344-9453). They are open 8 am - 8pm and can give you the number to a local branch of US Fish and Wildlife which can assist you with your search. www.fws.gov/

Or you can try calling - a veterinarian who cares for birds, or your local animal shelter. Also, your local zoo or aviary may help you find a rehabilitator and depending on the type of bird they may even take it.

Australia

Foundation for Natural Parks and Wildlife- this site has a very comprehensive rehabber list for all states. http://www.fnpw.org.au/resources/wildlife-carer-arescue-groups-australia

Oz Animals.com- lists rehabbers by State. http://www.ozanimals.com/wildlife-care.html

Wild Care Australia- Emergency hotline: 07 5527 2444 http://wildcare.org.au/rescue-information/

Wildlife Preservation Society of Queensland- a list of Queensland rehabbers. http://www.wildlife.org.au/wildlife/livingwithwildlife/rescue_and_care.html

Wildlife Victoria- Emergency Response line: 13 000
94535 http://www.wildlifevictoria.org.au/contact-us

Canada

Alberta Wildlife Rehabilitators' Association

Lists a number of rehabbers within this province.

http://www.albertawildliferehab.org/

Province wide wildlife helpline 1-888-924-2444.

Ontario Wildlife Rescue

This site has an interactive map which shows centers in
Ontario- when you click on a map location it tells you the
phone and website info for each rehabber.

http://www.ontariowildliferescue.ca/wildlifecentres/

Phone: (416) 436-9892

Rescue me- Rescue Shelter.com- This is a good list of
Canadian rehabbers http://wildlife.rescueshelter.com/ca

Wildlife Rehabilitators Network of British Columbia- this site has a good list of BC rehabbers.

http://www.wrnbc.org/links/ Phone: (250) 847-5101

Wildlife Rehabilitation Information directory
http://wildliferehabinfo.org/Contact_Intnl.htm#CAN
ADA

UK

British Wildlife helpline- This website has a very comprehensive rehabber list.
http://britishwildlifehelpline.com/centres%20_%20England .html.

Helpwildlife.co.uk - rehabber list
http://www.helpwildlife.co.uk/northwest.php

RSPCA has four rehab centers - which are located in Cheshire, East Sussex, Norfolk and Somerset. http://www.rspca.org.uk/adviceandwelfare/wildlife/findare habilitator. 0300 1234 999 (24-hour helpline)

Selby Wildlife Rescue- has a list of Yorkshire rehabbers. http://www.selbywildlife.co.uk/

Tiggywinkles wildlife hospital- 01844 292292 (24 Hour Emergency Line) http://www.sttiggywinkles.org.uk/

UK Animal Rescuers - has a list of UK rehabbers. http://www.animalrescuers.co.uk/html/wildcents.html

Wild About Britain - also maintains a rehabber list. http://www.wildaboutbritain.co.uk/forums/general-wildlife/5886-wildlife-rescue-centres.html.

International

Wildlife International – This is an amazing site which lists animal rehabbers for every country.
http://www.wildlifeinternational.org/EN/public/emergency/emergencyrehab.html

Wildlife Rehabilitation Information Directory- This site also lists rehabbers by Country.
http://wildliferehabinfo.org/Contact_Intnl.htm

Wild song birds (unless they are a house sparrow, starling or domestic pigeon), are protected under the Migratory Bird Treaty Act (1918) and it is illegal to keep them as pets!

There are thousands of wonderful animal rehabbers out there- the above list focuses mainly on rehabber lists, rather than individual rehabbers, in order to help narrow the search, so people can quickly find, and get help for injured or orphaned wildlife in their local area.

CHAPTER 2

(Figure 3) Baby resting on a planter by Sabine Fischer (2007)

IF YOU CANNOT GET THE BIRD TO THE REHABBER

There is a clause in the Migratory Bird Treaty called *The Good Samaritan Clause* which states that "you do not need a permit to pick up a bird in distress if it is taken directly to a rehabilitator (USFWS, 2013)." So that is your goal to get the bird to a rehabilitator as soon as possible.

Unfortunately, some people may be required to drive the baby three hours or more to the nearest rehabber. This is not always immediately possible if it is at night or during inclement weather.

Therefore, some US states like California have amended the Good Samaritan Clause with their own state codes. The California Code of Regulations # 679 states:

"Injured, diseased or orphaned animals may be temporarily confined by persons if they notify the nearest regional office of the department within forty-eight (48) hours of finding or confining such wildlife. Notification shall include name and address; the species of wildlife and a description of its injury, disease or condition; the date and location the wildlife was found; and the location where the wildlife is confined. Confined animals must be disposed of pursuant to department direction, which may include placement in a department approved wildlife rehabilitation facility (CCR, 2014)."

If you are unable to get the baby to a rehabilitator (within the US) be sure and report to US Fish and Wildlife immediately that you found the bird; and provide to them the above information; and why there is a delay getting to a rehabilitator. Fish and Wildlife may know of a closer rehabber or another option available to you.

Similar laws may apply in other countries- so you should ask your local rehabber who to contact if there is a delay getting the bird to them.

CARING FOR THE BIRD

(**Figure 4**) Indigo bunting eating by Lucinda Choules

If you are unable to get to the rehabilitator immediately; call US Fish and Wildlife (or other authority if you live outside the US) and notify them of the delay. If they state that it is ok to care for the bird overnight. Below, are some tips to help the baby survive the night.

Be advised though, internal bleeding is common with babies that have fallen out of tree nests. If this is the case with the bird you are caring for; despite your best efforts you may still lose the baby.

If the bird has an external injury and is bleeding; try to get it to the veterinarian immediately. If it is after hours and you cannot get the baby to the vet; wash the affected area off with soap and water. If the bird gets wet in this process dry it off with a hair dryer set on low. Be sure and keep the focus shifting constantly.

Do not focus the hairdryer directly at the bird or it could be burned; remember it does not have feathers to protect it from the heat. Instead, move the dryer around in a circular motion at a distance from the bird. Baby birds will die if you leave them wet or cold. It is very important to keep them dry and warm. Apply antibiotic cream to the affected area once the bird is dry.

Place the baby bird in a box or plastic storage bin; and fill it with shredded paper towels. The paper towels give the baby something soft to sleep on, and shredding the paper towels makes it easier for the baby to climb around. It is best to put the baby in a cup-like container so that it has support like a nest and surround it with shredded paper towels. You can also add small twigs and leaves so it feels more like home.

The baby will get out of this nest periodically so this small container should be inside of a larger box or a plastic storage container. Thus, when the baby gets out of the nest-like container, it is still in a safe place. Baby birds look completely helpless but they are still able to climb.

Be sure and place the large container/box somewhere safe- thus, if the baby escapes from the big container; he will not be hurt by a fall. For instance, do not put this container on a high shelf or on top of the fridge.

If you have a pet cat; the bird should be kept in a room that is not accessible by the cat. Your cat will assume that the baby bird is a present for him and actively hunt and try to eat the baby bird! It is not a good idea to leave your cat or dog alone in the room where the baby is located, even for a few minutes.

It is very important to keep the little bird warm; so get a heat lamp, heat rock, or heating pad. Ensure that the baby bird can move out of the heat if it is too hot. You can tell if the bird is too hot because it will start panting.

If you are using a heat lamp, ensure the baby can move around and always leave half of the enclosure unlit so the bird can get out of the light if it needs to. Be careful not to direct the light at elevated paper towels as this could start a fire. Put flat whole paper towels under the light and put the shredded towels outside of the light.

I have found heating pads are very good at keeping the baby warm but they do not get as hot as other heat sources so they are less dangerous and easier to work with.

(**Figure 5**) You can see a pink heating pad under the baby mockingbird below.

WHAT TYPE OF BIRD DID YOU FIND?

Now, take a close look at the baby bird - is it a songbird? Or a pigeon/dove? Songbirds will be almost naked with just some tufts of fluff. Songbirds often will have bright yellow or another color surrounding their beak. Pigeons or doves except when they are very small, will have a lot more feathers and look like small versions of the adults. Caring for a pigeon or a baby dove is much harder than a songbird.

If your bird is not a pigeon/dove or songbird, and has large eyes, claws and a very sharp beak, it is likely a raptor which is a meat eater. Do not feed the recipes enclosed in this e-book to raptors. If you have no choice but to care for the baby overnight, you could feed it small pieces of uncooked steak or chicken (no hamburger or bones) soaked in water.

Of course there are many other types of birds out there but if you find one in your yard, it is often one of these three types of birds. If your bird does not look like these birds, describe it to the rehabber or Fish and Wildlife representative so that you can figure out what to feed it.

(Figure 6) Baby owl, note- that it has large eyes and a sharp beak

Photo by - PublicDomainImages

(Figure 7) Baby doves resemble mini adults.

Photo by Debbie D (2012)

(Figure 8) Baby songbirds- have a colorful beak and lack feathers.

Photo by Gellinger (2014)

WHAT TO FEED THE BABY

MORE IMPORTANTLY, WHAT <u>NOT</u> TO FEED THEM!

While earthworms and caterpillars are good for the baby; mealworms and other biting worms are dangerous! Maggots can attack the baby by crawling into injuries or openings in the body such as the ear canal where they are difficult to remove, can invade the brain, and may kill the baby. If the baby has maggots in an injury. Fill a container with water and add liquid dish soap. Submerge the injured part – maggots do not like soap and will come out of the baby.

NEVER feed baby songbirds bread soaked in milk! This is a death sentence for the bird. The milk and bread forms into a concrete-like substance within the crop which completely blocks the crop preventing movement of water and food into the animal, thereby killing the bird. It is very difficult for a vet to remove this impaction.

(Figure 9) Bread and milk - please do not feed baby songbirds this!

Photo by Jenna Scott (2014)

Baby Bird – Food Recipes

Songbird Fruit Recipe

Exact, Supreme, or other brand parrot feeding formula

Gerber mixed baby cereal

Baby food jars- bananas, apples, pears

Note- I use parrot feeding formula as a base for my recipes, because it contains vitamins and minerals which are important for rapidly growing baby birds.

This formula should be prepared in small amounts according to the directions on the packaging.

Then add a little dry flaked mixed baby cereal; just enough to boost the grains in the food; this addition should not thicken the mix a lot. Do not use the food if you accidentally make it really thick, it should be slightly runny pudding-like in consistency when you are done.

Finally, add a tablespoon or two, of the fruit baby food (from the jar) and thoroughly mix.

Songbird Beef Recipe

Parrot feeding formula

Gerber mixed baby cereal

Baby food jars – beef wet cat food

The parrot formula should be prepared in small amounts according to the directions on the packaging.

Then add a small amount of mixed baby cereal in order to boost the grains in the food; this addition should not thicken the mix a lot.

Do not use the food if you accidentally make it really thick it should be slightly runny pudding-like in consistency when you are done.

Finally, add a tablespoon of beef baby food and/or a tablespoon of wet cat food then thoroughly mix. Please stay away from chicken-based wet cat foods and dog foods.

Songbirds – you can also soak dry cat food or dog food in water until it is soaked through.

CHAPTER 3

HOW TO FEED THE BABIES

(Figure 10) Juvenile scrub gaping in release cage

Song Birds

Baby songbirds that are weak will not gape for you initially. Gaping simply means to open up their mouth with an expectation of being fed; as the baby scrub jays in this chapter are demonstrating.

Before feeding, put the baby in a cup-like container to create a nest and fill it with shredded paper towels. The paper towels help support the body and neck so that the bird can hold up its neck in order to feed.

In order to get the bird to gape, there are a couple tricks to try - you can try making a short one or two note squeaking noise by whistling at the baby. Or, you can move your finger above its head in a wriggling motion.

Note- if the baby is dehydrated or weak; it may not gape no matter what you try. Therefore, you may want to give the baby some sugar water a half hour before you try to feed it; to rehydrate and energize it.

Since it will not gape; you will have to open the beak a little and with a dropper or a syringe, put one drop near the tip of its beak. Be careful though; because if you get water in the bird's airway it can aspirate to death. If you accidentally put too much water in and some gets in its airway it will make a panting-like gesture opening and closing its beak trying to breathe. There is some hope for the baby, if you immediately turn the chick upside down - this empties some of the water out of the mouth and airway. However, if there is too much water in there it will be fatal. Therefore, your goal with the water is to administer just a drop to reenergize the bird; not a whole syringe-full.

Note- *the above method can also be used to save an adult bird that is choking. When, I was living in Australia, my pet chicken "Fluffy" started choking on a large piece of corn cob that unbeknownst to me the manufacturer had added to the feed. I immediately turned her upside down and shook her gently, and the corn cob just popped out of her mouth onto the ground. Luckily she was fine. I immediately switched to a different brand of feed.*

Once the baby is gaping it is easy to feed; and it will likely open its beak every time you make a squeaking noise or even look at it directly. Baby birds respond to sound and will gape when they hear you come in to the room or approach their enclosure.

Make sure the food is warm, not cold! Do not feed cold food directly from the refrigerator to baby birds, this will make them sick and could kill them.

You can heat the food up in a microwave or saucepan; but be sure and test it on your hand before you feed it to the baby. If it is hot on your hand put it in the fridge until it cools to a warm temperature. Do not feed food that is hot to the touch; it will burn the baby's delicate crop.

(Figure 11) Baby scrub jay gaping. Note- the round plastic container inside of larger container with shredded paper towels.

When a bird is gaping there is much less chance of aspiration, as they are expecting someone to drop stuff into their beak. But, you still have to be careful how much you give them at once. Usually 1 cc is fine; possibly 2, depending on the size of the bird. Or you can feed one spoonful at a time; if you could not find a syringe at the feed store.

Please note- spoon feeding is much messier then using a syringe. So you and your walls will end up wearing a bit of baby food with this method.

When giving the bird food, make sure the bird has completely swallowed the first amount of food before giving him another. If you look into his mouth when he is gaping you can see if the food is still there or partially still there; so wait until it moves into his crop before giving him another spoonful. Also, you will want to keep an eye on the crop which is the sack-like thing in his neck. Be careful not to fill that too full or he could aspirate or throw up food.

I recommend feeding a little extra water mixed in with the first couple of spoonfuls or syringe feedings. The food contains water but it is good to give the bird a little extra. With songbirds I generally feed them Songbird Fruit first and then Songbird Beef the next feeding and repeat. If you want to, you can throw in a soaked cat food or dog food feeding as well. Leftover food should be immediately refrigerated in a container with a lid. Leftover food should only be reused a couple times before making a new batch. All wet food ingredients should be kept refrigerated.

Try and keep the baby at about 80 degrees particularly overnight. Do not expose to drafts or the bird could die.

Doves or Pigeons

For feeding pigeons and doves, I mainly just feed the Songbird Fruit recipe with extra mixed grain baby food. About once a day, I will also feed the Songbird Beef recipe. It is very hard to get soaked cat food into their mouth as they will not gape; so I would not recommend trying to feed soaked cat food to pigeons or doves.

As noted above, doves and pigeons do not gape, so feeding these birds is a lot harder. You will have to open the beak and squirt about half of a syringe into the little guys' mouth which is hard as aspiration is a concern.

Rehabilitators have more specialized tools for feeding these birds so you should do everything possible to get them to a rehabilitator quickly.

Still you can succeed at this type of feeding if you administer small amounts at a time and keep a careful watch on the crop to make sure it is not too full. Also add extra water to a few of the feedings. This extra water is important since they cannot drink on their own yet.

Rehabbers feed baby songbirds and doves every 20 minutes all day but not at night. This often is not feasible for other people, due to child and work commitments outside of the home. Instead, feed them every 2 hours in the day and every 2-3 hours overnight. Feeding overnight is important for single baby birds as they are less likely to feel abandoned; which could cause them to give up and die.

At a rehabber, they are surrounded by multiple baby birds so they are much less likely to feel alone or abandoned overnight. Moreover, since they have been fed every 20 minutes all day, they have the food resources to make it through the night.

(Figure 12) Below- a baby dove that I was raising, is keeping her friend a baby gallinule warm. Doves are very gentle and teenage doves are excellent foster mothers. She helped me raise the baby gallinule who I am holding in Figure 13.

IN CONCLUSION

Hopefully, with these tips you will successfully get the little bird through the night and to a rehabilitator for long term care. Rehabilitators care for orphaned birds all season; and they have vet staff available who can treat the babies. Moreover, rehabilitators have flight cages in which to house the baby birds once they start to fledge their wings. Birds that are raised by humans cannot be released immediately. Instead, they must stay for a couple of months in a release cage outside. The release cage gives them the opportunity: to watch wild birds search for food, interact with other birds, and learn socialization skills.

(**Figure 13**) The author in release cage for Florida rehabber surrounded by the birds she raised.

Thank you for caring about baby birds and how to help them!

I hope this guide book helps you one day when a family member walks into the living room carrying a baby bird that they found in the yard.

ACKNOWLEDGEMENTS

Thank you to all wildlife rehabbers - for working tirelessly to ensure that wild animals are treated with care, dignity and kindness.

Thank you to the talented and wonderful photographers from Pixabay.com whose work is showcased here.

Thank you to Office.com for their wonderful clipart.

Thank you to Jenna Scott and Elizabeth Arnold!

Thank you to WRR, Kendalia, TX and Rascals Wildlife Care, Florida.

PHOTO REFERENCES

Cover Photo by **Gwen Bailey** (2009) http://pixabay.com/en/birds-baby-house-wren-animal-101609/

Figure 1- by **Brigitte Werner** (2012) http://pixabay.com/en/red-robin-chick-young-bird-animal-181368/

Figure 2 - by **Deluna** (2012) nest http://pixabay.com/en/the-nest-bird-the-beak-kos-341928/

Figure 3- by **Sabine Fischer** (2007) http://pixabay.com/en/bird-young-animal-feather-382759/

Figure 6- by **PublicDomainImages** baby owl http://pixabay.com/en/fly-off-take-ready-if-as-perched-386923/

Figure 7 - by **Debbie D.** (2012) baby doves http://pixabay.com/en/birds-nest-tree-172099/

Figure 8 - by **Gellinger** (2014) baby blackbirds http://pixabay.com/en/bird-s-nest-blackbird-bird-breeding-341322/

Figure 9 –by **Jenna Scott** (2014) bread and milk- Thank you for providing this photo at short notice. You are a truly a great friend!!!!!

Figures – 4, 5, 10, 11, 12 and 13 by the author **Lucinda Choules**

CLIP ART

Office.com - all of the clip art and the cartoon baby bird are from office.com.

REFERENCES

(1) **US Fish and Wildlife Service** (2013) Migratory Bird Treaty Act of 1918. http://www.fws.gov/laws/lawsdigest/migtrea.html

(2) **US Fish and Wildlife Service Midwest Region** (2013) Good Samaritan Clause. http://www.fws.gov/midwest/migbirdpermits.htm

(3) **California Code of Regulations** (2014) Laws and regulations relating to abandoned and injured wildlife. **http://www.fgc.ca.gov**

www.ingramcontent.com/pod-product-compliance
Lightning Source LLC
Chambersburg PA
CBHW050858290526
45792CB00002B/642